ANIMALS AROUND THE WORLD

ALL ABOUT AFRICAN
OKAPIS

Robert Scally

Creating Young Nonfiction Readers

EZ Readers lets children delve into nonfiction at beginning reading levels. Young readers are introduced to new concepts, facts, ideas, and vocabulary.

Tips for Reading Nonfiction with Beginning Readers

Talk about Nonfiction
Begin by explaining that nonfiction books give us information that is true. The book will be organized around a specific topic or idea, and we may learn new facts through reading.

Look at the Parts
Most nonfiction books have helpful features. Our *EZ Readers* include a Contents page, an index, and color photographs. Share the purpose of these features with your reader.

Contents
Located at the front of a book, the Contents displays a list of the big ideas within the book and where to find them.

Index
An index is an alphabetical list of topics and the page numbers where they are found.

Glossary
Located at the back of the book, a glossary contains key words/phrases that are related to the topic.

Photos/Charts
A lot of information can be found by "reading" the charts and photos found within nonfiction text. Help your reader learn more about the different ways information can be displayed.

With a little help and guidance about reading nonfiction, you can feel good about introducing a young reader to the world of *EZ Readers* nonfiction books.

Mitchell Lane
PUBLISHERS

2001 SW 31st Avenue
Hallandale, FL 33009
www.mitchelllane.com

First Edition, 2020.

Author: Robert Scally
Designer: Ed Morgan
Editor: Sharon F. Doorasamy

Names/credits:
Title: All About African Okapis / by Robert Scally
Description: Hallandale, FL :
Mitchell Lane Publishers, [2020]

Series: Animals Around the World
Library bound ISBN: 9781680203950
eBook ISBN: 9781680203967

EZ readers is an imprint of Mitchell Lane Publishers

Library of Congress Cataloging-in-Publication Data
Names: Scally, Robert, 1958- author.
Title: All about African okapis / by Robert Scally.
Description: First edition. | Hallandale, FL : EZ Readers, an imprint of Mitchell Lane Publishers, 2020. | Series: Animals around the world-Africa animals | Includes bibliographical references and index.
Identifiers: LCCN 2018028571| ISBN 9781680203950 (library bound) | ISBN 9781680203967 (ebook)
Subjects: LCSH: Okapi—Africa—Juvenile literature.
Classification: LCC QL737.U56 S325 2020 |
  DDC 599.638096—dc23
LC record available at https://lccn.loc.gov/2018028571

Photo credits: Freepik.com, cover: Wendell Clendennen/ EyeEm, Getty Images, Shutterstock.com, mapchart.net

CONTENTS

Okapis are **rare**. They live in a **rain forest**.

Okapis are shy. They like to hide. Hiding keeps them safe.

Okapi fur is brown. The okapi looks like a horse but with white stripes on its legs. The stripes look like **zebra** stripes.

Okapis like to live alone. Female okapis stay with their **calves.**

11

Male okapis have two hairy horns. Females do not have horns.

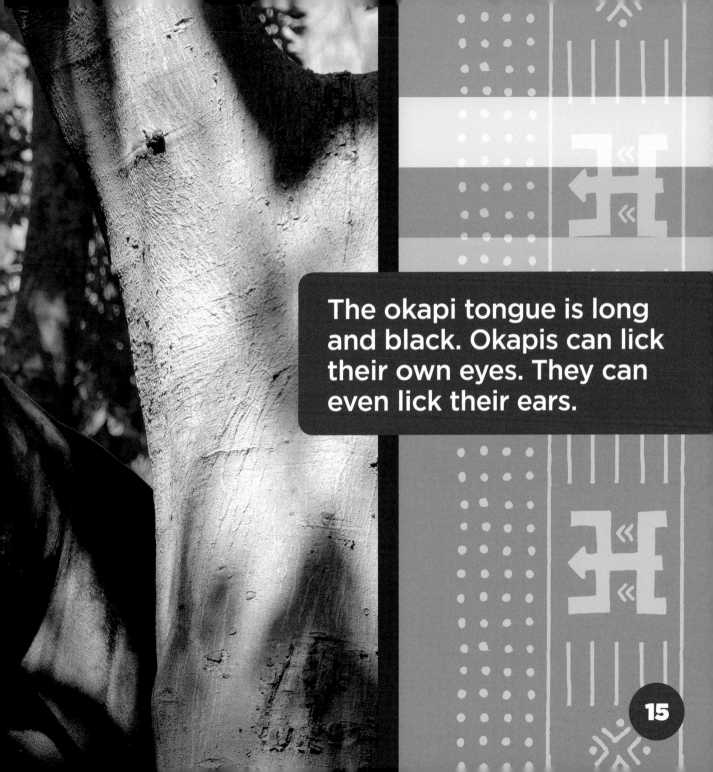

The okapi tongue is long and black. Okapis can lick their own eyes. They can even lick their ears.

Okapis eat leaves, buds, and grass.

17

Most okapis are born during heavy rainfall. New plants grow during the rainfall.

Female okapis make noises people cannot hear. They use the noises to find their young.

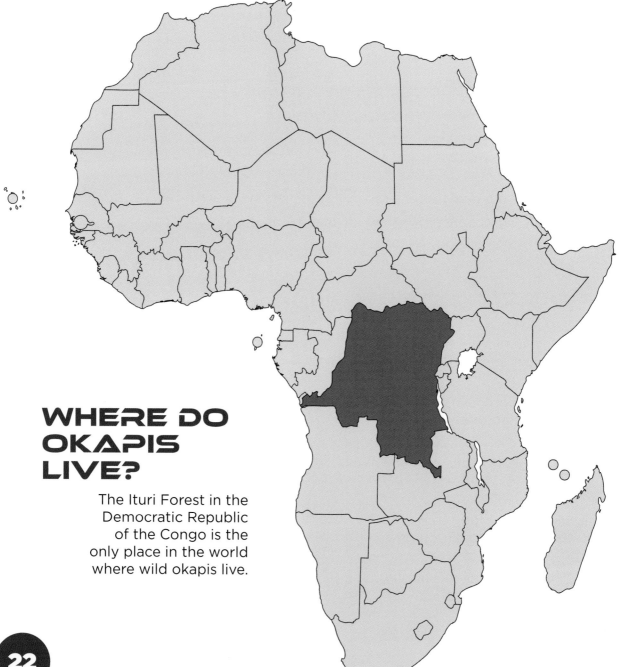

WHERE DO OKAPIS LIVE?

The Ituri Forest in the Democratic Republic of the Congo is the only place in the world where wild okapis live.

INTERESTING FACTS

- Okapis are the only relative of **giraffes**.
- Giraffes and okapis walk in the same way. They move both legs on one slide forward at the same time. Other animals with hooves move alternate legs on either side when they move.
- Okapis are plant eaters. They like tree leaves. They will also eat grass.
- The okapi's only natural enemy is the leopard.

PARTS OF AN OKAPI

Ears
Okapis have large flexible ears. They have good hearing. Females can make and hear sounds that humans cannot.

Legs
Okapi's legs have white strips on them. The stripes look like zebra strips. The stripes help them blend into the rain forest.

Horns
Male okapis have small horns on their heads. Females do not have horns. They have two bunches of hair instead.

Tongue
Okapis have long tongues. They use their tongues to eat tree leaves. Their tongues are so long they can lick their owns ears.

Neck
The necks of okapis and giraffes are similar. Both animals have seven bones in their necks. A giraffe's neck bone is bigger, making it much taller.

GLOSSARY

calves
Young okapis

giraffes
Animals with long necks that live in Africa

rain forest
Forests in warm climates with tall trees, and lots of rain

rare
Not often seen

zebra
An animal like a horse known for its black and white stripes

FURTHER READING

Ganeri, Anita. *The Story of the Okapi*. Chicago, IL: Capstone, 2016.

Lindsey, Susan Lyndaker, Green, Mary Neel, and Bennett, Cynthia L. . *The Okapi: Mysterious Animal of Congo-Zaire*. Austin, TX: University of Texas Press, 1999.

ON THE INTERNET

The Okapi Conservation Project
https://www.okapiconservation.org/

San Diego Zoo. Okapi - San Diego Zoo Animals & Plants.
http://www.animals.sandiegozoo.org

INDEX